Smart Sales
Methods that Really Work

By Alex Kampl

Smart Sales

ISBN-13:
978-1720340317

ISBN-10:
1720340315

Being a good seller is a super skill that can be developed if desired.

Not everyone can do it, since not everyone can afford to change their stereotypes regarding sales as a universal code of interpersonal communication and improve sales skills throughout life, regardless of occupation.

Content

Chapter 1 – Overcome your fear (forming of the confidence)
Chapter 2 – Psychology of sales or How to learn selling
Chapter 3 – Mistakes
Chapter 4 – Active and Passive Sales
Chapter 5 – 22 reasons why people buy
Chapter 6 – 25 rules of a successful seller
Chapter 7 – Art of sales
Chapter 8 – Epilogue

Author Page

Are you ready to sell everything to everyone?

Successful sales do not requires any secrets. All information is clear and easily accessible for everyone. The thing is that not everyone is ready to go to the end, to make it to the TOP and make money by selling!

I have made a lot of mistakes and lost numerous customers and my reputation, before I made my first $1,000 in sales. However, eventually I made it. Even though my products are more expensive than those of my competitors, yet MY people come back to me, because they are simply "comfortable" working with me. They feel secured!

What is the secret?
There are no secrets. Every seller has to follow certain rules, skills and intuition. Do you want to know more? Let's keep going ...

Index

> *At the end of the day, people laugh at their fears.*
> Paulo Coelho

> *Fear keeps a man better than all walls.*
> Haruki Murakami

> *No fear. No distractions. The ability to let that, which does not matter truly, and* slide.
> "Fight Club"

I believe you have faced it already. The fear! That is what holds you back and prevents you from being successful. I used to have the fear too, but luckily, I have overcome this feeling. It does not exist anymore.

If you have already got rid of the fear, you can proceed with the next chapter — Chapter 2.
If not, sit down and listen!

Chapter 1 – Overcome your fear (forming of the confidence)

A successful seller should have a lot of skills. However, nothing will work, if the person is not confident. What are the causes of insecurity and how to cope with it?

One of the main issues that beginners in sales business are dealing with is the lack of confidence. Why only beginners? If the seller remained in this field and therefore gained experience, then he or she had overcome this shortcoming and moved on. If a person did not manage to overcome the self-doubt, then, as a rule, he or she as leaves the business, as it causes discomfort, making it impossible to become an experienced seller.

Non-confident sellers are bad employees. They have low performance and experience personal disappointment. There is a good chance of them leaving a company, having failed to overcome insecurity.

As a result, the seller is struggling, feeling discomfort, constant tension, lack of development, frustration and has an intention to quit the profession. In particularly hard cases, the worker develops strong repulsion for the seller's profession. Probably that is why there are only few of just good sellers, who managed to overcome their uncertainty, and thousands of those, who got disappointed. The latter are those who keep saying that sales is a kind of business they will not ever do again.

In the meanwhile, **overcoming self-doubt is the key to the seller's personal development**, the development as a businessperson, entrepreneur; it's a development directed towards goals with no boundaries.

Self-doubt is a very complex and multifaceted problem that has many causes. A large number of people in the past has contributed to our feeling of self-doubt in both direct and indirect way, as it makes it much easier to manipulate us. Yet, we are coping with the result of their destructive influence during our whole life. It is better to understand this and get rid of this load as soon as possible, so that to stop it from holding us back on our way to accomplishment of our goals.

Since self-doubt is a multifaceted problem, **there are numerous ways of eliminating it.** To figure out how to overcome it, you first need to understand the deep nature of this problem, its origins, and then use the right tools for its "treatment."

Obviously, in this case self-doubt is not beneficial. Simply imagine an insecure warrior to predict what kind of results he or she will achieve and whether it will be enough to fulfill the task set by the management (sales plan). Therefore, we should **work on our confidence.**

The trouble spot is internal causes (personal, psychological). Survey conducted among sellers of my communication circle indicates that it is necessary to answer the question: "Is the person engaged in suitable kind of business?" Maybe professional sales is just not his or her thing. A well-known saying goes: "never try to teach a pig to sing." A person can be a good musician or teacher, but in that case, one does not need to engage in sales.

Another reason is **ignorance, undervaluation of the importance of sales for any business** and its role as an elite warrior, who is at the forefront of the attack and gets revenue for the company - source of its existence and development. This position is often typical for business executives, who are basically "tech guys", who arrogantly view sales as a side process of the business.

The next reason is undeveloped skills due to **the lack of sales experience.** This problem has the easier solution, as it can be eliminated by eventually turning the number of actions into their quality. Nevertheless, when starting a career in sales, the lack of experience, of course, affects the seller's confidence. One cannot make up for the lack of confidence just by faking it, which is rather typical trait of the beginners in sales.

Another vast area of self-doubt causes is **fears of any kind**. It is a great matter for discussion. There is no secret that we all have many phobias. It can be fear of failure, fear of success, fear of big money, fear of the new.

What kind of fears are causing a seller's self-doubt?
It is the fear of communication and communicating with people in order to make a sale. This is often expressed using phrases like "I do not want to

impose," "I do not want to foist." It indicates the seller's wrong attitude towards the profession.

Another one is the fear of failure and that the transaction will not take place. It is commonly perceived as a mistake, followed by a punished since school time. For this reason, people prefer to remain inactive so that they could avoid failure. As a result, the deal is lost, which intensifies the seller's feeling of disappointment.

A common reason for the lack of confidence is simple **ignorance concerning the sales toolkit** - methods, techniques, techniques. Thus, improper technologies and sales tools in the work are being used. This makes a seller act randomly, the way he or she likes that leads to a person's low efficiency, disappointment and passive attitude.

Poor knowledge regarding the selling product is another typical reason that causes seller's self-doubt. Inability to fully understand what you sell, the features of the product, or not quite sure about the information you have results in inability to demonstrate how the product meets the client's needs, and the way it benefits the customer. Therefore, percentage of rejections grows and so does gradual believe that the product is indeed bad and nobody needs it.

Understanding of all these reasons for the emergence and existence of the seller's self-doubt gives the key to overcoming it.

1.1. Sellers confidence forming

Let's consider **the factors that influence forming of the seller's self-confidence.** One could write a separate article about each of them. Therefore, we will go through them using "large strokes" to outline the general direction where to look for the answer to the question in the title of the article.

The first factor.
The right approach in personnel selection for the position of sellers. To be more specific, it is the owner's approach, which relieves one of the problem of confidence issue at the initial stage.

There are many methods that allow you to determine with some degree of certainty if applicants are suitable for sales, have the appropriate skill set, and psychological attitudes to regular communications aimed at achieving the result. In my opinion, it is necessary to distinguish the so-called "processional" and "productive" aspects of the psycho-type of the future seller, and therefore aimed primarily at the process and the result. Otherwise, your processional team can end up having someone, who enjoys communication as a process and gives completely unsatisfactory results in the form of sales revenue, because subconsciously its their priority.

The second factor.
Sufficient knowledge about the business as a system of value generation and the belief that the seller is the most important link in the company. It is a consequence of the understanding that sales are the engine of any business, as only sales bring money to the business, and everything else is an expenditure. Therefore, sellers are resource-earners for the existence of business, and the remaining employees are their dependents.

The idea that sales are the most important link that the company depends its existence on, should be daily broadcast by the head of the company to all personnel of the company. If the owner is a "tech guy", he or she will have problems with it. It is much better if the owner of a business is a seller essentially. In this case, the chances of instilling the right attitudes of thinking in sellers, gathering a team of like-minded people and creating a full-fledged sales-oriented company are much higher.

The third factor.
The right psychological attitude. It develops out of an understanding of the following fact: all that we do in communication with others is the essence of sale. In other words, we are all sellers, no matter if we are aware it or not. This does not necessarily involves money. We sell ourselves, our opinion, we negotiate, etc. "Selling" approaches are applicable to all kinds of communication situations. Since we are already engaged in sales, it makes sense to do it well.

Anyone, who understands this and consciously improves the sales skills, gets all the benefits, unlimited income, independence and freedom. The one, who denies that he or she is engaged in sales, as a result sells worse. Such a person is doomed to struggle with internal restrictions, dependence on better sellers, has to constantly conceal their fears under a veil of hypocrisy. Eventually, this leads to blocking one-selves from development and induces the causes of self doubt. In other words, we have no choice, and we must learn to sell, if we want to achieve a satisfying result.

The seller is always an individuality, not someone in "gray area". Therefore, if a person is not ready to become an individual, he or she blocks their development as a seller. Instead, if a person is looking for the ways to manifest their personality, they may need to think about a career in sales business.

The seller is a synonym for a successful person, businessman, entrepreneur, who decided to take 100% responsibility for their life. It is no accident that the first advice given by experienced entrepreneurs for beginners in business is to learn how to sell. All great entrepreneurs were primarily sellers.

The fourth factor.
Knowledge of human psychology, the way people make decisions. This is what competent communication with the client depends on. The seller should understand that it is him or her, who leads in a "sale game", which is, in fact, a communication, aimed at the making a deal. You can use the "hunter" approach, where you know what you do, you do it right, and eventually the world gives up and gives you a trophy. It's difficult to imagine an insecure hunter, isn't it?

The handbook of any seller, revealing the secrets of the way a client makes a purchasing decision , is R. Cialdini's Psychology of Influence. It makes sense to regularly reread the book and monitor the way described things work in practice.

The fifth factor.
Understanding of sales as a technological process that boils down to a set of described and regulated actions. It does not require creativity from the seller. If it is done as instructed, it leads to the result in the form of sales and income. Here it is necessary to know the "sales funnel", your indicators in the "sales funnel" (lead generation, lead conversion, repeat sales).

The head's task is to show that the sales process is formalized and regulated in compliance with technology. The lack of internal "optimization" at the seller level always leads to the certain result. It is necessary to get clear understanding of the relation between the set of well-regulated actions and the personal income of the seller. Then the process of sale turns from creativity into adherence to technological regulations, where it is difficult to imagine an insecure worker performing strictly regulated operations.

The sixth factor.
Regular training of sales managers for elaboration of effective working methods, tools, sales technologies, development of their communication skills, which constitutes the sales technique, aimed to prevent a worker of becoming a primitive advertising agent, spreading information about the product and facing a high percentage of failures, exacerbating inner self-doubt.

The main skill that sellers need to obtain is asking questions in order to understand the hidden problems of customers and translating them into customers' obvious needs. Nowadays, best tool for this purpose is the method of SPIN sales by N. Rackham, which should be known by every respected seller.

The seventh factor.
Learning about product. It is always necessary to understand what we sell from the point of view of the client. We need to be able to present the characteristics and features of our product (which the inexperienced

seller usually extols), in the language of benefits for our client. This involves the skill of figuring out what are the benefits for the client. An experienced seller has the skill of finding out the problems of the client, translating them into obvious needs and demonstrating how these or other features of the product satisfy these needs.

Factor eighth.
Practice and experience. This is increasing the number of actions that leads to the transition of quantity into quality. While increasing the number of actions, you should not be afraid of increasing number of errors that may follow. We were taught to be afraid of mistakes, and being punished for the wrong answers since school. Fear of making a mistake is the main thing to form self-doubt. It's keeping us from actions, when finding the right answers requires making mistakes and further corrections.

In order to learn sales and get rid of self-doubt, you need to increase the number of errors, make them as quickly as possible and to find out the right answers - what works and what does not. Use the "rule of 50 meetings": in order to acquire reinforced confidence in communicating with customers, you just need to hold a minimum of 50 meetings, with no regard for the outcome.

Proper goal setting is also of a great importance. The task of the head is to show the seller that the desired level of the income is requires the seller making the minimum number of actions that, through the sales funnel, will lead to the desired result. It is important to correctly treat the negative result of the next action (the absence of a deal) as an integral part of the sales process that brings the deal closer. The more rejections, the closer the deal.

The ninth factor.
Proper hiring management, training and the work of sales personnel is a factor that depends on the head of the sales department or the top manager of the company responsible for sales. The main approach here is that sellers should not be left to their own decisions, as sales processes should be regulated. Here, the only requirement for a manager is that he or she must understand that sales are a technology that to equip the sellers with and motivates them to perform the required actions while controlling them.

The factor is the tenth.
Correct organization of the sales department in the company. We are talking about the introduction of a three-unit sales department, which consists of the department of lead generation (marketing, attraction of potential customers), the department of lead conversion (sales) and the department of account management (repeat sales). Each of the units is an autonomous part of the technological process and consists of selling personnel of the appropriate qualification.

Such division of the sales department reduces the activity of sellers to the actions that are actually necessary at this stage. The seller improves one skill at a time (searching for potential customers, making a deal, making maximum repeat sales with the maximum frequency). The seller's self-doubt is eliminated so that he or she can effectively perform any operation, which increases the productivity.

<u>To sum up:</u>

- ❖ seller's self-doubt is one of the main problems that stop the development of a novice seller. The good news is that this problem can be solved;

- ❖ the key to solving the problem of seller's self-doubt lies in understanding of its causes. They can be both internal (in the area of personal psychological attitudes of the seller), and external (in the area of the social environment, which forms these settings). Ultimately, we always work with the head of the seller, with the content of his personality, and we can adjust it in the needed direction;

- ❖ when problems are diagnosed, they can be eliminated by forming correct psychological attitude of the seller, education regarding sales techniques and product, developing communication skills and maintaining the required level of activity that ensures the transition of quantity into quality. The more we play, the more we win. The more we win, the better we play;

- ❖ the person responsible for sales in the company can help the seller become more experienced by giving the right direction to his or her actions. But the final decision to develop, eliminating self-doubt, is always made by the seller.

Chapter 2 – Psychology of sales or How to learn selling

Why are you interested in psychology of sales? Do you want to learn how to sell? Make more sales? Does your income depends directly on this skill?
When I asked myself this question, I had to go through a ton of information.

Among the many information sources and paid trainings regarding this topic, I believe I found the most practical scheme of sales psychology. Every time my managers and I use it, selling becomes easier. Buyers don't stand a chance, they are ours!

The first rule of sales psychology: The one, who knows and pays attention to the motivation of the buyer, is the one to make a sale.

Buyer's or customer's motivation is the main component of the sale. The buyers pay not for the product, but for the result! They pay for solving their tasks and problems.

Something is pushing them to buy. In order to sell them a product, you need to understand what exactly pushes them.

There can be two kinds of psychological reasons:

1. Avoiding an unpleasant experience.
2. Desire to get a pleasant experience.

In psychology, it is called direct *motivation for* and *reverse motivation*. Let's see an example.

I want to rest! I want to go on a vacation. There I will be sunbathing, swimming in the ocean; meet new people maybe even find my destiny.

Reverse motivation: I want to go on a vacation! I am sick of my job, home and family. I am sick of all this.

Think of the last three things you bought.

Think of what have driven you to make those purchases. Was it direct or reverse motivation? A little later, you will understand why you are doing this.
Let me use an example with clothes to illustrate kinds of motivation in the psychology of sales.

Why do people buy clothes? Of course, you may assume that they need them only for protection from the sun, rain or snow ... but it was this way a long time ago. Nowadays there are many types of motivation for buying clothes.
There can be hundreds of reasons. Here are some of them:

— to look attractive
— for an important event
— nothing else to wear (with this one a person won't admit this fact if asked)
— to be more attractive for someone else
— for work
— because the significant other insisted
— to find something to go with new shoes
— to renew the wardrobe

As you can see, there are enough reasons for motivation. One may have a couple of reasons to motivate the purchase, yet only of them can be dominant.

If the seller fails assume the right reason, the probability of making a sale will be next to minimal. The potential clients will have to persuade themselves that the choice they have made was right and the seller will lose credibility.

Why do you need to know the motive of the purchase?

It will allow you better understanding of the clients. Consequently, you will be able to 'get in their shoes' and your offers will be more relevant for the solution of their task.

SCHEME IN THE PICTURE (HERE)

Here we will see a scheme that will lay it all out for you, help you learn how to sell, and increase your sales by 2-5 times. This is a scheme for writing marketing texts. The scheme used by the gurus of Internet marketing.

1) Pain + more pain (adaptation – we are one blood)

Let's say, we figured out that the motivation of our customer is the desire to please her boss, who is 35 years old, and he invited her to dinner. The right thing to say would be the following:

Do you want him to like you? Do you want him to be unable to take his eyes off you? (Yes, she does it and for her it's a pain, then you can tell your story, how you won attention, it's important to tell a true story, otherwise you risk losing your credibility.)

Now imagine the motivation of your client, whom you know. What questions will hit the target? What would hit the sore spot?

Feel free to ask questions like that! You will see the result in 10 seconds on a client's face. You can repeat those questions at least every 2 minutes. They will be very relevant for a customer and a him or her smile. A person will feel you understand him or her! And is it very important.

2) Solving the problem in general (what others do?)

Let's get back to our customer.

We can say things like that only if the buyer's choice is actually successful, and not because you need money and you want to make a sale:

Many customers look at the dress, try it on, and then leave to other store... but then come back and buy it. For some customers it takes a couple of days.

(Note: it's a common selling experience.)

Or:
Yes, it costs a lot, but many people try to save money and end up buying a thing that falls apart after the second wash.

Here we create push to the thoughts like: "Other people are stupid, but I'm not like that."

3) Our own solution (bullet points and profit)

You can buy this dress and it will serve you long. Wearing such a thing will be more pleasant experience, than wearing a cheap one. (If the price plays major role for the customer, this argument will be important). The men at our store are already looking at you. You will look good in this dress with both shoes and boots.

It goes good with black, gray and white colors. (This will work if a customer wears clothes of these colors).

4) Guarantees

The basis of the psychology of sales is that people always have doubt making a purchase. Giving guarantees, you will increase the amount of sales. You should always say it to a buyer!

You can always return the dress within 14 days, provided that it will not be worn and has the labels. We will refund the full amount.

Percentage of returns might increase, but it will not increase significantly comparing to the sales.

5) Gifts and free goods

Also, in addition to doubts, the human brain works in such a way that it starts to dissuade its owner, makes him or her doubt. Like: "It will have to go back, so far ... and this means losing time ..."

You should urgently give the brain a gift! Thus, we concretize the benefits, guarantees and do not leave any chances to this "harmful organ" :)

> Think of the ways to implement the mentioned above in your sphere.

Do you have an idea? Let's proceed with the psychology of sales:

6) «Sell the price» (explain why and how it's beneficial)

It's a triple strike! What can be better?

The main benefit for the customer in this case is to please the boss. We can either catch this moment, or miss it. Let's go for it:

This dress made of material X, which is quite expensive itself and also it has very good quality, can go through 100 washes. In addition, given the quality of tailoring, you are buying this dress for a ridiculous price. I am sure your significant other will appreciate the way you look in it. (This phrase will hit the aim, since you know the motive.)

7) How to get it (clear instructions)

Psychologically, the client is has been ready to buy it for a long time now. Now it is important to give her clear instructions on what to do to make a purchase.
Go to the register to buy the dress, make a payment and come back to me with a receipt.
Key points:

The idea of psychology of sales is that if you are not being sincere in your conversation, flattering or something, no sales psychology will help. First, try to help the buyer to solve his or her task! Moreover, if the product does not fit, it is better not to make a sale, than "foist".

Chapter 3 – Mistakes

Here follow the most common errors in sales that managers make in the sales of complex industrial equipment and, for example, sales assistants at a phone store or an auto parts store. At most part of the companies it's enough to look closely at your sales people and work on their sales mistakes with them to eliminate inefficient behavior patterns and improve sales.

Mistakes in sales №1 – Not knowing your product

At the company to make a successful sale sellers need to know the offered product; it is the ABC of sales. The technical characteristics of this super expensive piece of metalware that the company sells, how much it weighs and how long it is, whether it consumes a lot of diesel and how quickly it pumps 100 tons of oil through that rusty pipe.

If the seller has learned all the characteristics of the turbine or machine that he or she sells, it, of course, will give more confidence during negotiations with the client, but will not help much in sales, because first the customer needs to understand how he or she can solve a particularly painful problem using your product.

A customer needs to know how this piece of hardware, software or audit service, that your managers sell, will help to solve the problem at their company. In other words, to know that you are selling. First of all, it's understanding of the client's business and how your piece of metal can help this business cut costs, earn more money, or attract more buyers. Apart from that, just by itself the piece of hardware, software or audit is not needed.

Mistakes in sales №2 - Not selling oneself

There were such golden times when the seller had a product no one else had. Unfortunately, these times are long gone (maybe you will be surprised, but even a large Russian company Gazprom has competitors).

Your product, the client can buy in a hundred more other places and the Internet is a great help in it. The mistake the sales managers do is first selling the product or the company, although the first thing they need to sell is themselves, their expertise and only then the product.

It is necessary to show the client that the seller is an expert, who understands the client's business, its problems and knows how to solve them.

Only after the potential client has made sure that this manager is the person who has the necessary experience and knowledge in solving problems that are similar to the client's problem and can really help, only after that you can go for selling your product.

Mistakes in sales №3 - Desire to be right

Quite often managers are passionately defending their point of view, proving to the client wrong. Usually such a dialogue turns into confrontation and then into the failure to make a sale.

Do not argue with the client trying to persuade to change the opinion or prove your point. You need a sale, not a medal "I'm right!" Therefore, you just need to agree that the customer is entitled to have their own opinion, and move on together to a common goal, which is solving the client's problem by purchasing your product or service.

Mistakes in sales №4 - Skipping researching stage and going straight to the sales instead

The most common mistake in sales for most sellers is to start selling immediately. Such a seller is always ready for the battle and at the sight of the client immediately attacks him or her with stunning offers.

This mistake in sales an immediate transition to a presentation of the benefits, skipping the stage of identifying needs without asking at the beginning of the conversation. Therefore, a seller does not really know what benefits this particular customer. Sales manager like this is in great danger of failing to make a sale and usually has problems with the implementation of the sales plan.

Mistakes in sales №5 - Talking with anyone, yet not with the one who makes the decision

Trying to sell a product to someone who does not have money, to someone who does not dispose of the company's money is a mistake in sales. These people are ready to listen to the manager and even become sincerely interested in the product, but the problem is that they have no money.

Therefore, at the beginning of the first communication situation with the client, whether it is a call or a meeting, it is necessary to find out if the person can make a decision on buying your product or not, in other words, whether the person is in charge of making decisions or not.

Mistakes in sales №6 - Selling without an emotional component

Nowadays relying on the sales only based on the uniqueness of the product and the competitive advantages of your company, even though it worked well before, is a mistake in sales. "Why?" you may ask.

Mostly, no matter what your company sells, there are no monopolists left on the market, and you for sure have competitors. Both, the competitors and your manager, they all talk to the client about the same, naming the same set of advantages of working with them (which may not actually be true, but the client will not find out about it until later after learning about their product or service the hard way).
So, there is a pretty much the same product that one can buy in different places, there is also a set of quite similar competitive advantages stated by both, you and your competitors, and there is a confused client, who needs to choose one from the list of the same companies to make a purchase.

Help the client choose from your company among 10 identical other ones (in a client's subjective view). To do this, you should add emotion, positive drive to your sale, make the sale emotional (just do not go too far).

Your manager's motional sales will add color to the black and white picture. The idea of your company in the head of the client will have bright colors. It will allow the client to choose one colorful picture - your company,- among 10-20 identical other companies.

Mistakes in sales №7 - Talking too much, listening too litte

It's a mistake when a manager talks more, than a customer does. Every word can leave less and less chances of a manager guessing the client's actual needs. the same way the seller can hit the sore spot and thereby ruining the sale.

Your sellers will have more opportunities to make a profitable offer and sell your product or service, if the customer is the one to speak first. And if the manager asks the right questions and is able to listen to the answers given, then the client will tell the reason for buying. Then he seller will only have to mention the benefits and get money from the client.

Mistakes in sales №8 - Not being ready for the meeting

According to the statistics, only 19% of sellers prepare in advance for the upcoming meeting with the client. They collect information about the company's business and its decision-maker, they know the problems of the client's targeted industry.

The rest 81% of sellers neglect the preparation stage and make a mistake in their sales. For their companies it turns into low sales rates every month, and for the sellers it means living off fixed salary with no commision.

Mistakes in sales №9 - Failing to meet expectations

The formula is very simple. EXPECTATIONS OF THE CUSTOMER minus the CUSTOMER'S IMPRESSION equals to SATISFACTION OF THE CUSTOMER.

This means that whether the customer will be satisfied or not depends not on what you actually did, but on the picture of what should look like that the client got in his or her head. And your role is to help this picture coincided with what a person saw in reality, when the product is bought and tested.

Experienced sellers will never promise things they will not be able to do. Making such a mistake in sales and deceiving the client's expectations, will not let them make a re-sell with that customer.

Mistakes in sales №10 - Selling the product, not the benefits for the customer

Generally, the client does not care how many years your company has been on the market and that your engineers are super professional and covered with certificates, like trees covered with leaves. A customer does not care about the technical characteristics. All that a person is interested in, is what he or she will get, what exactly is the benefit.

Different clients need different benefits. Different people from the same company have different needs as they are different people and you are selling to people, not to a company. The sale will be only made if if the sales manager knows how to connect the product features with the customer's benefits at the stage of presentation.

Mistakes in sales №11 - Lack of analysis of your own failures and successes

Every manager in every company has his or her own personal sales plan. It can be in millions in terms of money, tons, liters, meters, pieces etc. I made a plan - I got a bonus; I did not do it - get a fixed salary and might be fired soon.

If managers do not analyze their successes and failures in sales, they are making a mistake. Comparing two figures of successful sales and unsuccessful sales is a very important indicator for further client work planning, identifying weak spots in sales, which is worth working on next time. Next month it will result in more sales, more money in your wallet and a better mood.

A little conclusion

These are the typical mistakes of the sales manager in corporate and retail trade. To avoid them, it is important to learn the theory of sales, to practice the knowledge in live communication with clients, to develop an effective practical skill. If you are a leader, train your subordinates, implement marketing innovations, raise morale, do not pay attention to stereotypes and go ahead!

Chapter 4 – Active and Passive Sales

Every business owner, manager or sales director, strives to expand the customer base and make sure sales volumes are constantly growing. Even now, in the age of information technology, trading success depends primarily on sellers. These pillars of business have different names: sales experts, managers, advisers or sellers. Their task is to attract the client, make a deal and to turn the single time customer into the regular one.

WHAT IS THE DIFFERENCE BETWEEN ACTIVE AND PASSIVE SALES?

Depending on the specifics of the business, the competitive environment of the features of the product (service), sales can be divided into active and passive one. The difference lays not only within the stages of the sale. The nature of the active and passive sales is different. Passive sale involves a short consultation and transaction support. In active sales, it is important to establish correct contact, to identify the client's needs and prepare for the transaction.

1. ACTIVE SALES

The need of professional active sales managers has always been urgent. Nowadays, with economic recession and market oversupply, HR-personnel struggle to find professionals in this sphere. Active sales is an art. It's a mixture of psychology, gamble, race for leadership and high income. This work does not only come to simple communication with a potential client. A professional has to analyze company's competitors, identify their target audience. Prior to the first communication, it is necessary to answer the certain questions: what are the problems of the potential client, and how can you help to solve them.

Stages of active sales:

- Gathering information.

- Cold calls in order in identify a DMP (a decision making person) and people who can influence the DMP.
- Identification of needs. There are effective sales techniques that help to pinpoint the client's problem, goals and expectations in the most accurate way.
- Presentation. The manager has to present the information, emphasizing the ways of solving the problem.
- Objection processing. Answering the client's questions, doubts dispelling.
- Bargaining. There is an unspoken rule that if a manager was the first one to call a potential customer and offered cooperation, then the client has the right to bargain.
- Deal. Preparation of documents. Monitoring the implementation of contractual obligations.
- Client's feedback.
- Preparation of a new deal.

Working with a base of cold, warm and active customers, analyzing the sales funnel is of particular importance.
Contrary to a popular belief, making the first deal is not the main task. The goal of the activ seller is to work in such a way that the partner becomes regular. That he or she, with a certain periodicity, would bring money to the company. You need to be persistent, but not obtrusive.

TYPES OF ACTIVE SALES MANAGERS

In order to choose or train the right employee, it is important to understand that there is a certain classification of managers. It depends more on the features of the person's character.
All successful salespeople combine following personal qualities:

- Motivation towards high income.
- Determination.
- Positive thinking.

- Broad-mindedness. Desire to learn new things.
- Philanthropy
- The lack of fear of failure.

Many things depend on the way the active sales manager is perceived by the partners. There are three types of managers:

Consultant. All the information received is a specification. Clients tend to minimize communication with such a manager. At the initial stage of building business relations, almost all active sales managers act as consultants. The client can easily change the decision and refuse the services of a consultant. Calls from the manager of this type are accepted reluctantly. Employees, who have never been present during personal meetings, run high risk of remaining a consultant forever.

The presenter. The client can easily notice the charisma and emotional reaction of the manager. He or she is pleased to listen to the professional. The manager-presenter most often sells during a meeting. Talking about the product or a service, the presenter uses analytical data, emotions, interesting stories and anecdotes. The manager-presenter is able to make a lot of quick sales. The client will always wait for an interesting show. Once a client loose the usual emotion, he or she can change the partner.

Expert. It is the most productive type of managers for active sales. In order to become an expert for the client, a sales person must possess not only excellent knowledge of the service or product sold. The manager should have a great understanding of the economy, politics and other information regarding all matters of interest of the client. The partner trusts the seller and therefore tries new products and services; has an emotional connection with the manager; values both, business and personal, relationships. The expert is able of building long-term relationships with customers.

WHERE DO YOU NEED ACTIVE SALES?

The cost of active sales managers is higher than of other specialists. Their income consists of a small fixed salary and a commission percent from the sales made. Therefore, managers themselves are interested in making more deals. Often the manager's salary costs are compensated by means of reduction in advertising expenditures.

Active sales managers are required in industries with high competition: advertising, travel agencies, law bureaus, companies providing any other services. Representatives of wholesale companies carry out active sales as well.

2. PASSIVE SALES

On the one hand, passive sales are pleasant, as they do not imply a customer search. The buyers themselves come to the company with an already formed need to purchase the goods or order a service. There are no cold calls; the number of failures is minimized.

However, on the other hand, the manager has fewer tools to influence the outcome of the deal. In passive sales, there is no building of long-term relationships. The manager has no control over his or her own income. The income consists of a fixed salary and a bonus part. It is fair for the main part to remain unchanged.

Passive sales are all about openness, unobtrusiveness and friendly attitude towards the customer or the buyer. The manager should be friendly and competent. It is important that to help the client solve the problem right now and right here. Having once received a competent consultation, the client will come to the store again and again.

Stages of passive sales:

- Establishing a contact. It is very important that client likes you at first sight. That is why in passive sales the

appearance and charisma of the seller is very important.
- Identification of needs. Most part of clients come with an already formed need. On the part of the employee, it is important to listen to the client, ask all the necessary questions.
- Consulting. The salesperson should evaluate if the customer's option is suitable or it would be better to offer a similar product or service, and then make an offer based on the client's specificities.
- Check increasing. After the contact has been established and the client's problem has been solved, the manager can tell about the novelties and the available promo-actions of the company or the store. If the woman buys a coat in the store, it will be logical for the consultant to offer a flattering scarf or a bag.
- Making a deal.

Passive sales are interesting because of their short term, with no information about the client. The seller has to identify client's real needs, and offer a suitable option.
Passive sales are actively used in financial institutions, insurance companies, retail stores, real estate agencies.

The effectiveness of passive sales depends not only on the skills of sales professionals, but also on the level of awareness of the audience. In passive sales, it is required to pay great attention to advertising support of the business. In addition, the location of the office or store is important.

Regardless of the type of interaction chosen by management, it is necessary to carefully recruit employees. They need training, supervision and clear motivation. Sometimes even sales virtuosos are not able of leading and keeping customers of the company. Therefore, it is necessary to pay special attention to the quality and relevance of the product and be honest with your customers!

There are many sciences, and, to my point of view, selling is a science as interesting and complex than any other one. It requires serious researching, daily practice, and there are still large-scale discoveries to be made in it that will allow sales managers to be more effective. And those who will delve into this science first, will conquer the market and become its leader.

Chapter 5 – 22 reasons why people buy

1. People buy to be liked.
2. People buy to be appreciated.
3. People buy to be right.
4. People buy to feel important.
5. People buy to make money.
6. People buy to save money.
7. People buy to save time.
8. People buy to make work easier or more efficient.
9. People buy to be safe.
10. People buy to be attractive.
11. Also, people buy to be sexy.
12. People buy for comfort.
13. People buy to be different.
14. People buy to be happy.
15. People buy to be entertained or to have fun.
16. People buy to find out something.
17. People buy to be healthy.
18. People buy out of curiosity.

19. People buy out of convenience.

20. People buy because of fear.

21. People buy out of greed.

22. People buy out of guilt.

If you have noticed, all of the reasons above are emotional ones. When you try to help people solve some of their problems, try to help alleviate their pain, always remember about this list of reasons.

However, what about physiological needs, you will ask? What about the hunger and cold?

The given products, namely the basic necessities are sold under the special scheme of marketing 4P.

Here different niche is affected; it has completely different reasons for purchases, different needs, different goods that will be harder to sell, comparing to basic necessities.

Selling goods that satisfy the deep reasons of your customers, you should operate completely different tool and pushing absolutely at different buttons.

Therefore, you can not sell directly, you can not push the client. You should do it indirectly, within a certain context. For comparison: You do not sell pork steak, you sell the smell of this steak to attract the hungry passer-bys and tease the appetite and desire to buy and eat this tasty lump of meat.

Agree, having sensed the smell of fried pork, you will much more quickly want to taste it, rather than you will simply see a photo of the same steak on the road banner. And why? Yes because the smell affects your deeper, internal receptors more, than your visual perception.

That is why your texts should "put out" some particular pain of your reader, solve deep problems, satisfy your client's value needs (for example, get rid of acne, help with employment and money, etc.).

Also your texts should solve many additional problems. For example, having more money, you can realize the old dream of your kid - buy a bicycle or rollers. Being healthy and beautiful, you can easily meet new people and improve your personal life, etc.

While writing the text use these reasons, according to which, people buy this or that product, in order to achieve the desired result. And the goal, as we stated earlier, is selling, selling yourself, selling goods or services, selling information, selling a brand of a company, etc.

Chapter 6 – 25 rules of a successful seller

Do you want to be the very person that all the best employers are fighting for? If this is the case, you will have to learn, learn and learn again ... to sell. Sell yourself as the best specialist, your experience, success, projects, and ideas.

It is all about selling!
Maybe you was not born with seller's skill set. Maybe you have been brought up with the repulsion to commerce. Maybe the role of a seller does not excite you at all. But take a good look around. Nowadays selling skill is a universal skill that helps professionals from any sphere achieve actual success.

If you try to think of a "seller's antipode" in professional field, an "IT guy" would probably do. However, for example, Jay Gardner, CIO BMC Software, does not mention knowledge on the subject matter as the most important quality to help him in his work. It was experience in sales and marketing that helped him to take this post. "The organization already has 400 employees with excellent technical knowledge," says Gardner. "And the skills that CIO requires day after day are the same as I used in sales - building relationships, asking questions and listening, communicative skills, and the ability to persuade." According to a 2003 study by the State of the CIO, with 539 CIOs interviewed, 35% named the ability to sell and convince as the most important skill that ensures business success. In a similar study in 2006, CIO named communication skills (70%), the ability to think strategically (59%), and motivate employees (54%) as the most important ones.

Guru Tom Peters states that "for a talented person to survive in this inverted world, we all need to re-introduce ourselves ... as first-class sales professionals." There is no "thinking in the style of sales = no wow-projects = no survival. Full stop". Think about it, you already had to "sell" yourself during exams, at interviews, during presentations. Perhaps you think that a successful seller is a person with no principles, ready to do anything for the sake of selling. Listen attentively to the respected opinion of the most successful professionals in sales, talking about the helpful qualities in sales. There is a chance you might be surprised.

Selling personalities
According to Paul Johnson, founder of Panache and Systems LLC consults, whose sales career began in 1979, in addition to successful experience, a good salesperson must have such qualities as respect for others and self-esteem, innovativeness, determination and enthusiasm. A successful seller should enjoy helping the buyer, using the natural and acquired talents.

Omid Kordestani, senior vice president of global sales and development for Google, is a head of a 90-members sales team:

"When Google appeared in 1998, people were wondering why the world needed another search engine. We focused on demonstration of the value that the company brings to the lives of its clients and customers. The boom has passed. There can be no more mistakes or people, who do not know how to sell. Therefore, we carefully select our sellers. We have a complicated hiring process. In addition, we are careful with our customers. Before selling, we need to make sure that Google's solution is the right thing for the customer. If we do not believe that we can solve the problem of our client, we refuse to cooperate, even if the client is ready to make a deal. In the short term, it is a painful situation, but it is the right solution in terms of long-term prospects. For example, two years ago we gave up a multimillion-dollar contract, because our product at that time could not really solve the client's problem. Our competitor got the contract. We have improved our product, and our competitor failed to fulfill the promised. Now this client is working with us. "

Advice of Omid Kordestani: Do not make a deal until you are sure that you can solve the problem of your client.

Joseph Abruzzze, the head of sales of the Discovery channel, previously served as a president of sales of CBS Television:

"I have been a head of sales in CBS Television for 10 years. While selling commercial time, honesty is everything. We have about 80% of regular customers, with whom we work from year to year, and sales depend on the quality of our relationships. In the end, the honest agents win. One of the leaders of the television network, our competitor, once said that sellers do not have much shame. I strongly disagree. If one of our clients tells me that our seller has no shame, I will fire this employee. In a business based on relationships, our employees sell through honesty and creativity. "

Joseph Abruzzi's advice: Be honest.

Fred Bialek, co-founder of National Semiconductor Corp.:

"The sense of sales is to understand your client's needs and convince him or her that you are able to satisfy their need in the best possible way. Today, in the semiconductor business, a lot of people are trying to sell by the virtue of price. But the best way to sell is to sell by the virtue of value. It is harder because you have to use your brains. But this is the only way to succeed. In the 1970s, our "sales by the virtue of value" were similar to the work of a missionary. I had to convince large supermarket chains that they needed our systems. The only way to do this was to understand the business that they were doing. I learned the industry so well that presidents of retail chains often asked me for an advice. We have made fundamental changes in the work of supermarkets. If you use the brains and be persistent, you will really get something done. "

<u>Fred Bialek's advice: Strive to understand your client's business.</u>

John O'Bryant, a staff member of George Nahas Oldsmobile, who repeatedly won the title of bestseller:

"We do not pressure customers. We show a good product at a good price, and let them decide on their own. I work hard at effective listening. When a buyer appears, we talk about what he or she wants to talk about. It's amazing how many interesting things you can learn, if you just listen. For example, a husband and a wife went to the Lincoln Town Car five years ago. The wife have hated him for all five years, and her husband did not even know about it. My philosophy is: pay more attention to the customer, and you will be able to sell the car even to the biggest grumbler in the world. I know it for sure. He already bought three cars from me. "

<u>John O'Bryant's advice: "Learn how to listen carefully".</u>

Rules of successful sellers

Tom Peters in his book "Essentials. Talent" represents a collection of "rules", originally intended for the leaders of the sales team of a large high-tech company. Now these are the rules that will have to be followed by everyone, wishing to succeed.

1. Know your product. This tip is obvious, but worth stating (and not just once): you must be competent as hell in what you "foist"!

2. Know your company. Another truism (which does not mean that you will ever be able to let yourself to forget it): you sell your company to the same extent and even more than a product or service.

3. Know your client. Any form of legal intelligence - including (especially) personal juicy details - are worth your effort. Tip: until the "intelligence" has worked, do not even think about making the first call to your client!

4. Love politics. Axiom: sales is politics. "Politics" ... in the sense of "the way people work together to achieve results."

5. Respect your competitors. You can deeply hate them. Maybe for a reason. It does not matter. Do not put down competitors.

Full stop. Nothing puts you in a stupid position more than mudslinging a legitimate competitor.

6. Get in touch with the buyer organization. Establish close, warm relationships at all levels and in all structures of your enterprise-buyer.

7. Build connections within your organization. The buyer buys not so much the thing, but rather experience-production-and-after-sale-experience-of the product.

8. Therefore, the more and better you can show the multifaceted talents of your company in this matter ... the higher are the chances of making a deal, and even higher chances to repeat deal.

9. Never promise too much. Your future is always in question. And it is always completely dependent on your credit of trust.

10. Sell the solution. Sell only ... through certain problems and creation of profitable opportunities. Great sellers do not sell "things" (even "things that are so damn good"). They sell solutions. ("Solutions that are so damn good".)

11. Ask for help (and do not be too "proud" for this). Solving the problems of the buyers, expanding their abilities, deepening their experience, resort to all possible resources. "Resources" means "people". Including mortal enemies.

12. Live the history of the brand. Your company sells a "story". The story of "what it's like to do business with us." The story of our "vision", "the experience we offer", our "dream".

13. **Celebrate a "good failure". "A good failure" is a bold and daring effort, which for some reason has not reached its goal (yet).**

14. **Perceive every problem as your own. The problems of customers are your problems! For God's sake, never blame "logistics" for the late delivery.** Take full responsibility.

15. You will earn real money through repeated deals. Repeated deals are made thanks to the goods and services that you offer ... and also because of the tremendous and everlasting, constant impression from working with you. And this impression will as marvelous as you will make it.

16. Do not hold back the information. When a problem occurs and you are unavailable, you want the client to have a complete list of your employees who can fix the crash.

17. Get away from bad business. When you see that people in the buying organization are not trustworthy, when the "games" around the deal go much further than the normal political "tug-of-war", when the business becomes a trouble, you may need to gracefully (or not so gracefully) "quit it".

18. Do not whine about the price. It is normal to lose a customer because of the price. And yet ... one of the surest signs of the seller-going-nowhere is constant complaining that he or she" fails at sales because of the price."

19. Do not miss the slightest chance ... to do business. But ... be careful! I know too many cases, when sellers persuaded their organization to make absurd compromises in order to make a "first deal" with some "important client". They say: "Let's do it just one time. Later we can put our normal price." Moral of the story: once perceived as weak you will remain weak forever.

20. Respect the newcomers (the real enemy). A real enemy these days is rarely your "main competitor". It's more likely that it's a competitor-not-leaving-mark-on-the-screen-your-radar, but with a much better idea-that will seriously "harm" you in the coming years.

21. Look for "cool" buyers. During dramatic changes, it is essential that your client portfolio include companies "from the front line" - people, who are pursuing today features of excellence of tomorrow.

22. Say "partnership". The word "partnership" is used too often. My advice: use it anyways. This is exactly what you are selling.

23. Send letters of gratitude! Sales is a business of relationship. A good word is a powerful tool for strengthening relationships.

24. Make your customer a hero. When you look at the customer, ask yourself: "How can I make this guy rich and famous? How can I contribute to his (or her) advancement?"

25. Let your slides be simple. If you are in sales, sooner or later you use your good old Power-Point presentation. Therefore, keep these damn slides a few and full of info!

Set a goal to change-this-damn-world! Let's go back to the heartfelt cry of Apple Computer CEO Steve Jobs: "We're here to put a dent in the universe." I think the idea that selling can leave a dent in the universe is what keeps us motivated and able to look at ourselves in the mirror.

Nowadays we are all sellers. Foster the strong character of the seller. You have to sell your product (outside prospective). You should sell your project (inside prospective). You have to sell your talent (look from any prospective).

Chapter 7 – Art of sales

Selling is one of the most difficult professions to have in our world. Why? I will give you a simple answer. Just take look at the sales professionals at work. Look at the activities of a seller, achieving tremendous success in this field, and you will instantly realize how difficult it is to ensure sales in any business.

The art of sales is something that everyone is trying to get into, but only a few succeed in it. By success, I mean not selling a pack of chewing gum in an underground passage, but a truly worthy success with customers. If you apply this statement to your own online business, then success in sales means real income, sufficient to sustain your own financial independence and a desired lifestyle.

Mastering the art of sales can truly enrich you. But until the moment when your art will start to bring you a solid income in practice, you will have to sweat quite a bit and work very diligently. Unfortunately, the vast majority of training programs and sales trainings happen to have very common mistakes and do not save the entrepreneur from mistakes that he or she in no way should be allowed to do in sales.

Below, I want to show you something in order for you to understand that it is necessary to take the sales skill seriously. I will give you only 25 basic skills and 25 qualities and characteristics that an entrepreneur should have if he or she wants to succeed in sales. Carefully look through this list and mark a) what is missing in your professional arsenal, b) what you should work on; c) what needs some serious work to be done, and d) something that you never thought of.
I guarantee that the result will shock you.

Skills:

- listening;

- asking questions;

- setting goals;

- productive time management;

- effective planning;

- event scheduling and following the schedule;

- objectively evaluate and use the perspective;

- overcoming circumstances;

- computer skills;

- copyrighting;

- delivery of presentations;

- successful negotiation;

- working with any size of audience;

- usage of audio-visual tools;

- art of persuasion;

- completion of transactions;

- agreement;

- being well-dressed, having style and making a good impression;

- art of negotiations over the phone;

- being well-organized;

- finding mutual understanding;

- non-verbal communication skills;

- strategic planning;

- finance management;

- working with distribution networks.

Qualities and characteristics:

- active approach;

- calm reaction to a rejection;

- physical stamina;

- emotional steadiness;

- concentration;

- persistence;

- sympathy;

- determination;

- stress-resistance;

- ability to deal with ambiguity;

- balance;

- ability to recover from crises;

- self-respect;

- ability to remain hopeful;

- loyalty;

- the ability to put oneself in other person's position;

- flexible behavior;

- ability to adapt to innovations;

- adequate evaluation of the environment;

- problem solving;

- self-discipline;

- result-oriented attitude;

- analytic thinking;

- emotional maturity;

- ability to compromise.

Having studied this list of fifty items, answer me the question: Are you still surprised by the fact that the art of selling is a very complex skill?

Meanwhile, most entrepreneurs continue to believe that mastering the art of sales can be very easy. Imagine that you have to constantly face a lot of failures and be constantly vilified by the public. Will you manage to cope with this, become a winner in this situation, and endure it all and succeed despite everything? And what about working for 14 hours a day, regular meetings, negotiations, relocations, and no days off?

Of course, the art of selling is one of the greatest in nowadays world. It's one of the most respected, profitable and prestigious arts, but at the same time it is one of the most difficult to master. Although, this does not mean that it is impossible to learn this art.

Epilogue

There are many books and articles on the art of sales, but you can learn how to sell by taking into account only a few principles. The rest is a matter of practice. As in any other field, the longer a person is in sales, the better and more efficiently, he or she is able to do it.

Instruction

1 As for the basic principles of sales, there are very few of them - only 3. By following them, you can learn to sell anything, if you want to.

2 It is necessary to sell not goods or services, but solving a problem for a specific person. In other words, the product itself can be great, the service is effective, but the buyer will not want to pay money unless he or she is sure that the purchase will satisfy the needs. And there is no point in telling the person about the merits of the goods, as he or she will not buy it.

3 How can a product or service help a person solve problems? For example, when selling a ticket, the travel company sells the opportunity to have a good rest and rejuvenate or make new memories. When selling an apartment, the agent offers not just a room with certain characteristics, but a place where a person can rest or work, comfortable housing, where he or she will feel comfortable and secluded with their family. Any offer should start with the needs of the potential client, and a good seller, first of all, must answer the question: why is this particular product or service suitable for the person that I make an offer to?

4 People do not like to solving problems on their own, as well as thinking, and looking for solutions. If there is someone who offers them a ready-made solution to their problem, they accept it with joy and readiness. The more convincing the seller assures that the

purchase is a quick and quality solution to the problem, the more readily the buyer will purchase the offered product.

5 People like feeling their importance and rightness, so a good seller will not argue with the buyer, even if he or she is absolutely wrong. By agreeing with a potential buyer, starting any dialogue with recognition of a clients rightness and demonstrating an understanding of his or her doubts, the seller creates an atmosphere of trust. The task of a good seller is to bring the buyer to the idea that the product or service offered to buy is absolutely necessary. It will seem like a client made their own decision, and, therefore, will be internally pleased with a purchase.

Author Page

Good day to everyone!

My name is Alex Kampl and I am here to share my experience in different spheres. I was born and raised in Europe and that was where I went to school as well. My books are meant to educate people who strive to learn.

All the information is based on my own observations and experiences of my friends. I hope you will enjoy it.

www.ingramcontent.com/pod-product-compliance
Lightning Source LLC
Chambersburg PA
CBHW030037230526
45472CB00002B/547